THOMAS DEGAN

Coding with AI

Unlocking Productivity and Innovation in Software Development

First edition

This book was professionally typeset on Reedsy.
Find out more at reedsy.com

Contents

Introduction

Introduction: AI's Role in Modern Software Development

In the rapidly evolving world of software development, the tools and practices developers rely on have transformed dramatically over the past few decades. From manual code writing to powerful integrated development environments (IDEs), each advancement has aimed to make development faster, more efficient, and more accessible. Enter Artificial Intelligence— arguably one of the most groundbreaking innovations to reshape the landscape of software development.

AI isn't just a buzzword or a futuristic concept. It's a practical tool that developers, whether seasoned or just starting, can leverage to improve productivity, enhance code quality, and tackle challenges more efficiently. But let's get one thing straight: AI won't replace developers. Instead, it acts as a powerful assistant, augmenting human creativity and decision-making. The idea isn't about having AI do everything for you; it's about using it to supercharge your capabilities.

Why AI Matters to Developers

For years, developers have faced common pain points: repetitive tasks, debugging nightmares, and the ever-present challenge of meeting tight deadlines. AI tools can address many of these issues head-on. Imagine having an assistant that can:

- Generate boilerplate code in seconds, freeing you to focus on the core logic.
- Analyze codebases to identify bugs or inefficiencies faster than you ever could manually.
- Automate testing processes, ensuring higher-quality software with less effort.

These are just a few of the ways AI is already making an impact, and its potential is growing by the day.

Dispelling the Myths About AI in Development

There's a lot of hype—and fear—around AI's role in software development. Let's address a couple of the most common misconceptions:

1. **Myth:** AI will replace developers.
2. **Reality:** AI is a tool, not a replacement. Developers are essential for understanding complex problems, designing creative solutions, and making critical decisions. AI can assist but not replace this expertise.
3.
4. **Myth:** AI-generated code is flawless.
5. **Reality:** AI is only as good as the data it's trained on. It

can suggest solutions, but those solutions still require validation and fine-tuning by a skilled developer.

6.
7. **Myth:** Using AI means less work for developers.
8. **Reality:** While AI can automate repetitive tasks, it often shifts the focus to higher-order tasks, like optimizing AI outputs, ensuring integration, and maintaining quality.
9.

What This Book Will Teach You

This book isn't about building AI models or integrating AI into your applications. Instead, it's about leveraging existing AI tools to enhance your development process. By the time you finish, you'll know:

- How to choose the right AI tools for your needs.
- Practical strategies for incorporating AI into your work-flows.
- How to avoid common pitfalls and measure the impact of AI on your productivity.
- The latest trends in AI for software development and how to stay ahead of the curve.

Whether you're debugging a tricky issue, trying to write cleaner code, or simply exploring ways to work smarter, this book will guide you through the best practices and practical applications of AI tools tailored for developers.

The Road Ahead

The chapters ahead will cover everything from understanding what AI can do for developers to exploring specific tools and workflows. Along the way, you'll find practical examples and insights to help you get the most out of AI tools. Whether you're just starting or looking for ways to optimize your existing workflow, this book has something for you.

So, let's dive in and discover how AI can transform your development process—starting with what it can do for you today.

1

What AI Can Do for Developers

Chapter 1: What AI Can Do for Developers

Software development is a dynamic and demanding field, requiring a blend of creativity, technical skill, and problem-solving. Developers often juggle multiple responsibilities, from designing systems and writing code to debugging and maintaining software. AI tools have emerged as game-changers, designed to simplify, accelerate, and enhance these tasks.

In this chapter, we'll take a closer look at how AI tools are transforming the software development process, their capabilities, and their limitations. By understanding these, you'll gain a clearer picture of how AI fits into your workflow and how it can help you work smarter.

AI Capabilities in Depth

1. Code Generation

AI tools are particularly skilled at generating code, from simple snippets to complex functions. These tools rely on vast datasets of existing code to suggest solutions based on patterns they've learned.

- **Capabilities:** AI can write boilerplate code, create functions based on descriptive comments, and even scaffold entire projects.
- **Benefits:** Eliminates repetitive coding tasks, reduces errors in syntax, and speeds up development.
- **Examples:**
- A developer writing a web form in Python's Flask framework can simply describe the desired form layout in plain English, and an AI tool generates the necessary HTML, CSS, and backend code.
- Generating an authentication system, including user login and registration flows, by typing a few prompts.

2. Debugging Assistance

Debugging can consume a significant portion of a developer's time. AI tools streamline this by automatically detecting potential issues in your code.

- **Capabilities:** Identify syntax errors, suggest fixes for runtime bugs, and explain the cause of common errors.
- **Benefits:** Reduces time spent hunting for errors, particularly in large codebases.

- **Examples:**
- A developer gets an error related to a null pointer. An AI tool highlights the specific line of code, explains why the error occurred, and offers a fix.
- AI flags a performance bottleneck in nested loops and suggests replacing them with more efficient alternatives.

3. Testing Automation

Testing is critical to software quality, but creating and managing tests can be a tedious process. AI tools simplify this by automating test generation, execution, and even maintenance.

- **Capabilities:** Generate unit tests, analyze code for edge cases, and suggest test scenarios based on your codebase.
- **Benefits:** Speeds up the testing process, improves test coverage, and reduces manual effort.
- **Examples:**
- A developer working on a REST API can use an AI tool to generate a suite of test cases that validate the API's endpoints, parameters, and responses.
- Identifying untested edge cases by analyzing application behavior and suggesting additional tests.

4. Code Review and Optimization

Code reviews ensure that software meets quality standards, but reviewing large codebases can be overwhelming. AI assists by analyzing code for inefficiencies, detecting potential bugs, and suggesting improvements.

- **Capabilities:** Spot redundant code, suggest optimizations, and ensure adherence to coding standards.
- **Benefits:** Enhances code quality and ensures consistent practices across teams.
- **Examples:**
- AI identifies repeated blocks of code in different files and suggests creating a reusable function.
- Refactoring suggestions improve readability and maintainability, such as renaming variables for clarity.

5. Project Management and Task Prioritization

AI tools go beyond code by helping developers and teams manage projects more efficiently.

- **Capabilities:** Break down tasks, prioritize work based on deadlines, and analyze team productivity.
- **Benefits:** Reduces manual overhead in project planning, allowing developers to focus on coding.
- **Examples:**
- An AI tool suggests splitting a complex feature into smaller, manageable tasks and assigns them based on team members' expertise.
- AI predicts how long each task might take, helping the team create realistic timelines.

6. Knowledge Retrieval

Developers often rely on online searches or documentation to solve problems. AI tools provide quick, accurate answers to coding questions, saving time.

- **Capabilities:** Search and summarize documentation, provide code snippets, and explain concepts.
- **Benefits:** Reduces time spent researching and boosts productivity.
- **Examples:**
- A developer asks an AI, "How do I use a regular expression to validate an email in Python?" and receives a working example with an explanation.

AI in the Developer Workflow

Let's explore how AI integrates into various stages of the software development lifecycle:

1. **Requirement Analysis and Planning:** AI can help define project goals, create initial roadmaps, and prioritize tasks.
2. **Development:** AI assists with coding, debugging, and generating documentation in real-time.
3. **Testing:** Automated test generation ensures higher code quality and faster delivery cycles.
4. **Deployment and Maintenance:** AI monitors applications post-deployment, detects anomalies, and suggests fixes.

What AI Can't Do

Despite its strengths, AI is not a magic bullet. Developers should understand the limitations of AI tools to use them effectively:

- **Critical Thinking:** AI lacks the creative and contextual problem-solving abilities that human developers bring to projects.
- **Domain Knowledge:** AI struggles with niche or highly domain-specific tasks where patterns aren't well-defined.
- **Interpreting Business Needs:** Translating business requirements into technical solutions remains a job for humans.
- **Handling Complex Architectures:** AI-generated solutions may not consider broader architectural implications without human guidance.

Realizing AI's Potential

By automating repetitive tasks and enhancing development workflows, AI frees up developers to focus on what they do best: creating innovative, high-quality software. Whether you're debugging a tricky problem or brainstorming a new feature, AI is a reliable assistant to help you work faster and smarter.

As we move forward, we'll dive into the tools that make all this possible, starting with general-purpose AI tools for developers.

2

General-Purpose AI Tools for Developers

Chapter 2: General-Purpose AI Tools for Developers

Artificial Intelligence has created a wide array of tools aimed at improving software development processes. Among these, general-purpose AI tools stand out for their flexibility and versatility. Unlike domain-specific tools tailored for narrow tasks, general-purpose AI tools can be adapted to fit various aspects of the development lifecycle, from code generation to project management.

In this chapter, we'll explore what general-purpose AI tools are, their strengths and weaknesses, and practical use cases where they shine. By understanding how to effectively use these tools, you can unlock their full potential in your workflows.

What Are General-Purpose AI Tools?

General-purpose AI tools are designed to perform a wide range of tasks, making them suitable for many aspects of software development. These tools are typically powered by advanced AI models like GPT (Generative Pre-trained Transformers) and leverage large datasets to understand and generate text-based outputs.

Examples of general-purpose AI tools include:

- **GitHub Copilot:** An AI coding assistant that suggests code in real-time as you type.
- **ChatGPT or similar AI chatbots:** Useful for answering programming questions, debugging, or generating boilerplate code.
- **TabNine:** A code completion tool that integrates seamlessly into popular IDEs.
- **AI writing tools:** Useful for creating technical documentation or explaining complex code.

Key Features of General-Purpose AI Tools

Code Generation:

- Generate entire functions, classes, or snippets based on prompts.
- Adapt to your coding style over time.
- Provide real-time suggestions as you type in your IDE.

Code Explanation and Debugging:

- Offer natural-language explanations of how a specific piece of code works.
- Analyze errors or bugs and propose fixes.

Documentation and Summarization:

- Generate clear and concise documentation for codebases.
- Summarize lengthy sections of code to explain what they do.

Versatility:

- Perform multiple tasks without being tied to a specific domain, making them useful for everything from testing to deployment planning.

Strengths and Weaknesses of General-Purpose AI Tools

Strengths:

- **Flexibility:** Can be applied to a variety of tasks without the need for extensive configuration.
- **Ease of Use:** Designed to work with minimal setup, often integrating directly into IDEs.
- **Wide Application:** Suitable for coding, debugging, documentation, and beyond.

Weaknesses:

- **Context Limitations:** Struggle with tasks that require deep knowledge of the entire codebase.
- **Accuracy:** Suggestions may sometimes be incorrect or inefficient, requiring human oversight.
- **Learning Curve:** Understanding how to craft effective prompts or queries may take time.

How to Choose the Right Tool for Your Needs

Selecting the best general-purpose AI tool depends on your specific goals and workflow. Here are some factors to consider:

Integration with Your Workflow:

- Does the tool integrate seamlessly with your preferred IDE or platform?
- For example, GitHub Copilot is ideal for VS Code users, while TabNine supports multiple IDEs.

Task Complexity:

- Is the task straightforward (e.g., boilerplate generation) or complex (e.g., debugging)?
- Simpler tasks are well-suited for general-purpose tools, while complex tasks may require manual intervention.

Output Quality:

- Evaluate the quality of code suggestions and explanations. Some tools excel at specific languages or frameworks, so choose one that aligns with your stack.

Practical Use Cases for General-Purpose AI Tools

1. Code Generation

Scenario: A developer is creating a data processing script in Python.

Solution: Using a general-purpose tool like GitHub Copilot, the developer types a comment describing the function's purpose (e.g., "Parse a CSV file and calculate average values for each column"), and the AI generates the core implementation.

2. Debugging

Scenario: A developer encounters a runtime error in a JavaScript application.

Solution: Using ChatGPT, they paste the error message and relevant code into the chat. The AI analyzes the issue and suggests a fix, explaining why the error occurred.

3. Documentation

Scenario: A team is finalizing a library and needs user-friendly documentation.

Solution: The team uses an AI writing tool to convert technical comments into detailed documentation, complete with examples and explanations.

4. Task Automation

Scenario: A developer frequently repeats tasks like setting up project structures or configuring environments.

Solution: A general-purpose AI tool automates these tasks by generating templates or scripts, saving hours of manual effort.

Tips for Maximizing General-Purpose AI Tools

1. **Craft Clear Prompts:** Be specific about your needs. For example, instead of saying, "Write code for sorting," say, "Write a Python function that sorts a list of integers in ascending order using the bubble sort algorithm."
2. **Validate Outputs:** Always review AI-generated code for accuracy and efficiency. AI tools can make mistakes or overlook nuances.
3. **Experiment with Features:** Explore all the capabilities of the tool, from debugging assistance to documentation generation. You may discover features you didn't know existed.
4. **Iterate and Learn:** Use feedback mechanisms (if available) to improve the tool's understanding of your coding style or project requirements.

Conclusion

General-purpose AI tools are a cornerstone of modern software development, offering flexibility and power across various tasks. From code generation to debugging and documentation, these tools can significantly boost productivity when used effectively. By understanding their strengths, weaknesses, and use cases, you can seamlessly integrate them into your workflow.

In the next chapter, we'll dive into domain-specific AI tools, exploring how they specialize in addressing particular challenges in software development.

3

Domain-Specific AI Tools for Developers

Chapter 3: Domain-Specific AI Tools for Developers

While general-purpose AI tools are incredibly versatile, domain-specific AI tools excel in solving challenges tailored to particular aspects of software development. These tools are designed with a narrower focus, targeting specific tasks such as testing automation, performance optimization, or security auditing. By leveraging their specialized capabilities, developers can address intricate challenges that general-purpose tools might struggle with.

In this chapter, we'll explore the purpose, advantages, and limitations of domain-specific AI tools, highlighting scenarios where they outperform their general-purpose counterparts.

What Are Domain-Specific AI Tools?

Domain-specific AI tools are built to address specific challenges within the software development lifecycle. Unlike general-purpose tools, which can perform a wide range of tasks, domain-specific tools focus on excelling in one area. They often incorporate domain knowledge, such as best practices, industry standards, or pre-trained models for specific use cases.

Examples of domain-specific AI tools include:

- **Testim:** Automates software testing with AI-driven test creation and maintenance.
- **Snyk:** Focuses on identifying and fixing vulnerabilities in code and dependencies.
- **DeepCode (by Snyk):** Provides AI-driven code analysis with a focus on bug detection and optimization.
- **Launchable:** Uses machine learning to prioritize the most critical test cases to run in CI/CD pipelines.

Key Features of Domain-Specific AI Tools

Targeted Expertise:

- Built for a specific domain, such as security, testing, or deployment optimization.
- Provide highly accurate and context-aware insights.

Automation at Scale:

- Automate repetitive or time-intensive tasks within the targeted domain.
- Reduce manual effort while improving precision.

Domain-Specific Insights:

- Offer recommendations based on industry standards or best practices.
- Highlight issues that require immediate attention.

Strengths and Weaknesses of Domain-Specific AI Tools

Strengths:

- **Precision:** Tailored for specific tasks, offering more accurate and actionable results.
- **Domain Knowledge:** Often include built-in knowledge of industry-specific standards and guidelines.
- **Efficiency:** Streamline specialized workflows, saving time and effort.

Weaknesses:

- **Limited Scope:** Lack the versatility of general-purpose tools.
- **Integration Challenges:** May require additional effort to integrate into existing workflows or tools.
- **Learning Curve:** Understanding how to leverage the full potential of these tools can take time.

How to Choose a Domain-Specific AI Tool

When selecting a domain–specific AI tool, consider the following factors:

Your Needs:

- What specific problem are you trying to solve? For example:
- If you need security scanning, consider tools like Snyk.
- If testing automation is the goal, Testim might be more appropriate.

Integration:

- Does the tool work well with your existing tech stack, such as your IDE, CI/CD pipeline, or testing framework?

Accuracy:

- Evaluate the tool's effectiveness in solving the problem it's designed for. Look for case studies, reviews, or trial versions to assess its capabilities.

Scalability:

- Can the tool handle larger or more complex projects as your needs grow?

Practical Use Cases for Domain-Specific AI Tools

1. Testing Automation with Testim

Scenario: A QA team struggles to keep up with frequent code changes, leading to brittle and outdated tests.

Solution: Testim uses AI to automatically generate and update test cases, ensuring they adapt to changes in the application's UI or logic. This reduces manual test maintenance and improves test reliability.

2. Security Scanning with Snyk

Scenario: A developer adds a new library to their project but isn't sure if it introduces vulnerabilities.

Solution: Snyk scans the library for known vulnerabilities and suggests safer alternatives or patches, ensuring the codebase remains secure.

3. Prioritizing Tests with Launchable

Scenario: A CI/CD pipeline runs hundreds of tests, delaying feedback for developers.

Solution: Launchable uses machine learning to identify which tests are most critical to run based on recent code changes, significantly reducing pipeline execution time.

4. Code Analysis with DeepCode

Scenario: A large codebase has accumulated technical debt, making it difficult to maintain.

Solution: DeepCode analyzes the codebase for potential bugs, inefficiencies, and areas for improvement, providing actionable recommendations to clean up the code.

Tips for Maximizing Domain-Specific AI Tools

Understand the Tool's Focus:

- Dive into the documentation or tutorials to fully understand what the tool specializes in and how it can fit into your workflow.

Combine with General-Purpose Tools:

- Use domain-specific tools alongside general-purpose ones to cover a broader range of tasks.

Regular Updates:

- Ensure the tool is kept up to date, especially for areas like security scanning, where new vulnerabilities are discovered frequently.

Iterative Implementation:

- Start small by applying the tool to a single project or feature, then scale its usage as you gain confidence in its capabilities.

Conclusion

Domain-specific AI tools offer unparalleled precision and efficiency for solving targeted problems in software development. By focusing on specific domains such as testing, security, or code analysis, these tools help developers address challenges that require a higher level of expertise. Although they lack the versatility of general-purpose tools, their specialized nature makes them indispensable for streamlining specific aspects of the development lifecycle.

In the next chapter, we'll explore how to evaluate and select the right AI tool for your specific needs, ensuring that you get the most value out of these powerful technologies.

4

Selecting the Right AI Tool for the Job

Chapter 4: Selecting the Right AI Tool for the Job

With the growing number of AI tools available, selecting the right one for your specific needs can feel overwhelming. Each tool comes with its own strengths, weaknesses, and best use cases. Making the right choice ensures you maximize productivity and avoid wasted time experimenting with tools that aren't a good fit.

This chapter will guide you through the process of evaluating and selecting AI tools for software development, focusing on practical criteria and strategies to help you make informed decisions.

Why Choosing the Right Tool Matters

Every development team has unique workflows, challenges, and goals. An AI tool that works well for one team might not be effective for another. For example:

- A small team looking to automate code reviews might benefit from a lightweight general-purpose tool like TabNine.
- A security-focused project might require a specialized tool like Snyk to scan dependencies and identify vulnerabilities.

Choosing the right tool ensures:

1. **Efficiency:** The tool aligns with your workflow and enhances your productivity.
2. **Cost-effectiveness:** You get value for your investment, avoiding unnecessary expenses.
3. **Scalability:** The tool can grow with your projects as they increase in complexity.

Key Factors to Consider

1. Task Requirements

Start by identifying the specific problem you're trying to solve. This will narrow your search to tools designed for that purpose.

- **Questions to Ask:**
- Is the task broad (e.g., general code assistance) or specific (e.g., testing automation)?

- Will the tool need to integrate into an existing workflow?
- **Example:** If your primary need is generating unit tests, tools like Testim might be ideal. For general-purpose coding assistance, GitHub Copilot is a better fit.

2. Integration and Compatibility

The best AI tools seamlessly integrate with your existing tools, platforms, and workflows. Compatibility ensures a smooth user experience and avoids unnecessary disruptions.

- **Questions to Ask:**
- Does the tool support your preferred programming languages?
- Can it integrate with your IDE, version control system, or CI/CD pipeline?
- **Example:** GitHub Copilot integrates seamlessly with Visual Studio Code, making it an excellent choice for developers already using that IDE.

3. User Experience

A tool's usability determines how quickly you can get started and how effectively you can leverage its features.

- **Questions to Ask:**
- Is the tool intuitive and beginner-friendly?
- Does it offer clear documentation or tutorials?
- **Example:** Tools like ChatGPT are highly user-friendly, offering conversational interfaces that require little to no learning curve.

4. Performance and Accuracy

AI tools are only as good as the results they deliver. Evaluate their performance and ensure they provide accurate, high-quality outputs.

- **Questions to Ask:**
- How reliable are the tool's suggestions or outputs?
- Does the tool frequently generate incorrect or irrelevant results?
- **Example:** A testing automation tool should reliably create meaningful test cases without introducing unnecessary complexity.

5. Cost and Licensing

AI tools come in a variety of pricing models, including free versions, subscription plans, and enterprise licenses. Consider your budget and evaluate the cost-to-value ratio.

- **Questions to Ask:**
- Does the tool offer a free trial or freemium version?
- Are there hidden costs, such as limits on usage or additional fees for integrations?
- **Example:** While GitHub Copilot is subscription-based, it offers a free trial, allowing developers to test its value before committing.

6. Community and Support

A strong user community and responsive support team can make a big difference when you encounter challenges or want to learn advanced features.

- **Questions to Ask:**
- Is there an active community or forum where users share tips and experiences?
- Does the tool provide timely customer support for troubleshooting?
- **Example:** Tools like Snyk have robust communities and documentation, making them easier to adopt and troubleshoot.

Evaluating Tools Through Hands-On Testing

Even with research, nothing beats hands-on testing. Most AI tools offer free trials or limited-feature versions to help you evaluate their performance.

Steps to Evaluate an AI Tool:

1. **Define a Test Case:** Choose a small, manageable task that represents the kind of problem you want the tool to solve. Example: Generating a Python function, automating a test case, or scanning for vulnerabilities.
2. **Monitor the Results:** Assess the tool's performance in terms of accuracy, speed, and ease of use.
3. **Iterate:** Test the tool on a few different tasks to get a sense of its consistency and versatility.
4. **Involve Your Team:** If the tool will be used by a group, gather feedback from colleagues to gauge usability across skill levels.

Common Scenarios and Recommended Tools

Scenario Recommended Tools

Generating boilerplate code GitHub Copilot, TabNine
Debugging complex issues ChatGPT, DeepCode
Automating test creation Testim, Launchable
Scanning for security vulnerabilities Snyk, Checkmarx
Writing technical documentation ChatGPT, AI writing assistants

Tips for Making the Final Decision

1. **Prioritize Essential Features:** Focus on the features that directly address your most pressing needs.
2. **Avoid Overlap:** If you already use one AI tool, make sure new tools add value without duplicating functionality.
3. **Consider Long-Term Viability:** Look for tools with regular updates and active support, ensuring they remain useful as technology evolves.

Conclusion

Choosing the right AI tool is a critical step in integrating AI into your development workflow. By evaluating your specific needs, testing tools thoroughly, and considering factors like integration, cost, and support, you can make informed decisions that maximize productivity and efficiency.

In the next chapter, we'll explore how to measure the productivity impact of AI tools and ensure they're delivering tangible benefits to your workflow.

5

Measuring Productivity with AI Tools

Chapter 5: Measuring Productivity with AI Tools

Integrating AI tools into your workflow can dramatically enhance efficiency and quality, but how do you measure their impact? Without clear metrics, it's challenging to determine whether these tools are genuinely improving productivity or just adding another layer of complexity.

In this chapter, we'll explore practical methods to measure the productivity gains from AI tools, focusing on key performance indicators (KPIs) and strategies for tracking their effectiveness over time.

Why Measure Productivity?

Measuring productivity isn't just about justifying the use of AI tools—it's about understanding their value and optimizing their role in your workflow. By quantifying productivity, you can:

- Identify which tools are providing the most significant benefits.
- Uncover areas for improvement in your workflows.
- Justify investments in AI tools to stakeholders or team members.

For example, a team using an AI-powered testing tool might want to measure how much time it saves in generating and maintaining test cases, compared to manual testing.

Key Metrics for Measuring Productivity

Time Savings

- **What to Measure:** How much time is saved on specific tasks (e.g., code generation, debugging, testing).
- **How to Measure:** Track the time spent on a task before and after adopting the AI tool.
- **Example:** Developers using an AI tool for generating boilerplate code reduce coding time for repetitive tasks by 40%.

Code Quality

- **What to Measure:** The quality of code produced, including fewer bugs and better adherence to standards.
- **How to Measure:** Monitor metrics like:
- Bug density (bugs per line of code or per feature).
- Code review feedback (e.g., fewer rejections or corrections).
- **Example:** After introducing an AI-powered code review tool, the number of critical bugs discovered in production

decreases by 30%.

Test Coverage

- **What to Measure:** Improvement in test coverage and accuracy of test cases.
- **How to Measure:** Compare pre- and post-tool adoption metrics such as:
- Percentage of code covered by tests.
- Number of edge cases caught during testing.
- **Example:** An AI testing tool generates additional test cases that increase code coverage from 75% to 90%.

Error Resolution Speed

- **What to Measure:** Time taken to identify and resolve errors.
- **How to Measure:** Track average bug resolution time before and after using an AI debugging tool.
- **Example:** Debugging time for runtime errors reduces from an average of 4 hours to 1 hour with AI assistance.

Developer Satisfaction

- **What to Measure:** How developers feel about the tools' impact on their workflow and productivity.
- **How to Measure:** Conduct surveys or gather feedback from the team.
- **Example:** A survey reveals that 85% of developers feel less frustrated with debugging tasks after implementing an AI assistant.

How to Track Productivity Over Time

Baseline Metrics

- Start by establishing baseline metrics for tasks before adopting an AI tool. This will provide a point of comparison to measure improvement.
- **Example:** Record the average time spent on generating boilerplate code across multiple projects.

Monitor Usage

- Use analytics or logging features in AI tools to track usage patterns and identify areas of high impact.
- **Example:** An AI tool's usage report shows that 70% of developers use it primarily for debugging.

Iterate and Optimize

- Regularly assess the tool's performance and adjust its usage or configurations to improve outcomes.
- **Example:** If a code review tool flags too many false positives, tweaking its sensitivity settings might reduce noise.

Challenges in Measuring Productivity

1. Subjective Impact

Not all benefits are easy to quantify. For instance, the creative boost from using AI to generate ideas might not have direct metrics.

2. Team-Specific Variability

Different teams may experience varying levels of improvement based on their workflows, experience levels, or project complexity.

3. Initial Adjustment Period

There's often a learning curve when adopting new tools, which may temporarily reduce productivity before improvements are realized.

Case Study: Measuring AI Impact in a Software Development Team

Scenario: A team of 10 developers integrates GitHub Copilot for code generation and debugging assistance.

Baseline Metrics:

- Average time to write a new feature: 20 hours.
- Average time to resolve a bug: 6 hours.

Post-Integration Metrics:

- Feature development time reduces to 15 hours (25% improvement).
- Bug resolution time drops to 3 hours (50% improvement).

Developer Feedback:

- 80% of developers report reduced frustration with repetitive tasks.

- 70% feel more confident tackling unfamiliar technologies with AI-generated suggestions.

Conclusion: The team estimates that GitHub Copilot saves 120 hours of work per sprint, enabling faster delivery without sacrificing quality.

Tips for Maximizing AI's Impact

1. **Set Clear Goals:** Define specific objectives for each tool (e.g., reducing testing time by 30%).
2. **Regularly Review Metrics:** Periodically assess the tool's impact and adapt your workflow as needed.
3. **Encourage Feedback:** Continuously gather input from your team to identify pain points or areas for further improvement.
4. **Focus on Complementarity:** Use AI tools as a complement to human skills, not a replacement.

Conclusion

Measuring productivity is essential to fully realize the benefits of AI tools in software development. By tracking metrics like time savings, code quality, and developer satisfaction, you can ensure these tools are delivering tangible value to your projects. While challenges exist, a thoughtful approach to measurement can help you optimize tool usage and justify investments in AI technology.

In the next chapter, we'll discuss common pitfalls developers encounter when using AI tools and provide strategies for avoiding them.

6

Common Pitfalls When Using AI Tools

Chapter 6: Common Pitfalls When Using AI Tools

AI tools offer immense potential for boosting productivity and simplifying complex tasks in software development. However, like any tool, their effectiveness depends on how they are used. Missteps in adopting or relying on AI can lead to inefficiencies, inaccuracies, or even counterproductive outcomes.

This chapter explores the common pitfalls developers face when using AI tools and provides strategies to avoid them, ensuring you maximize the benefits of AI while mitigating risks.

1. Over-Reliance on AI

The Pitfall:

It's tempting to rely entirely on AI tools for tasks like code generation, debugging, or testing. However, AI-generated outputs are not always perfect and may lack the nuances or domain-specific understanding required for complex projects. Blindly accepting AI suggestions can introduce bugs, inefficiencies, or security vulnerabilities.

How to Avoid It:

- Treat AI tools as assistants, not replacements. Always review their outputs critically.
- Use AI for repetitive or straightforward tasks, reserving complex problem-solving for human expertise.
- Regularly validate AI-generated code against your project's requirements and best practices.

2. Misaligned Expectations

The Pitfall:

Many developers adopt AI tools expecting them to solve every problem or dramatically reduce all workloads. When tools don't meet these inflated expectations, frustration and disillusionment follow.

How to Avoid It:

- Understand the capabilities and limitations of each AI tool before integrating it into your workflow.
- Set realistic goals, such as improving efficiency by 20% or reducing debugging time for common errors, rather than expecting perfect solutions.

3. Poor Tool Selection

The Pitfall:

Using the wrong AI tool for a specific task can lead to inefficiencies and wasted resources. For example, using a general-purpose AI tool for domain-specific tasks like security scanning might produce subpar results.

How to Avoid It:

- Clearly define your requirements and evaluate tools based on their strengths, weaknesses, and suitability for your needs.
- Test multiple tools when possible, starting with free trials or limited-feature versions, to determine the best fit.

4. Ignoring Context or Project-Specific Needs

The Pitfall:

AI tools often make assumptions based on general patterns, which may not align with your specific project or domain. For example, AI-generated code might not consider edge cases or specific business requirements.

How to Avoid It:

- Provide clear, detailed input to guide AI-generated outputs. For instance, when generating code, include detailed comments or prompts about expected behavior and constraints.
- Ensure AI-generated outputs are adapted to your project's specific context through manual review and refinement.

5. Lack of Validation and Testing

The Pitfall:

AI-generated code, tests, or suggestions are sometimes implemented without adequate validation. This can lead to errors, inefficiencies, or even security vulnerabilities making their way into production.

How to Avoid It:

- Always test AI-generated code or fixes in a controlled environment before integrating them into your project.
- Perform code reviews to validate outputs against quality standards and business requirements.

6. Workflow Disruptions

The Pitfall:

Integrating AI tools without considering their impact on existing workflows can create friction. For example, if a tool doesn't integrate well with your IDE or version control system, it may slow you down rather than speeding things up.

How to Avoid It:

- Prioritize tools that integrate seamlessly into your current workflows and tools.
- Introduce AI tools gradually, allowing your team to adapt and identify any pain points early.

7. Security and Privacy Risks

The Pitfall:

Some AI tools process code or data externally, raising concerns about confidentiality and intellectual property. For example, uploading sensitive code to a cloud-based AI tool could inadvertently expose your project to unauthorized access.

How to Avoid It:

- Understand the tool's data handling policies and ensure they comply with your organization's security standards.
- Avoid uploading sensitive or proprietary data to AI tools that lack robust security measures.

8. Overloading Developers with Too Many Tools

The Pitfall:

Using multiple AI tools without clear boundaries can overwhelm developers, leading to confusion and inefficiency. For instance, overlapping tools might provide conflicting suggestions, causing unnecessary complexity.

How to Avoid It:

- Limit the number of AI tools in your workflow to those that provide clear, distinct value.
- Regularly evaluate your toolset and remove tools that offer redundant functionality.

9. Failing to Stay Current

The Pitfall:

AI tools evolve rapidly, and failing to keep up with updates or new features can limit their effectiveness. Outdated tools may miss new capabilities or improvements that address known limitations.

How to Avoid It:

- Subscribe to updates or newsletters from your AI tool providers to stay informed.
- Allocate time for your team to explore new features or tools periodically.

10. Neglecting the Human Element

The Pitfall:

AI tools are designed to enhance human capabilities, not replace them. Over-automation can lead to a loss of critical thinking, creativity, and team collaboration.

How to Avoid It:

- Encourage developers to use AI tools as collaborative partners rather than replacements for their expertise.
- Maintain a balance between automation and manual input, especially for tasks requiring creativity or deep understanding.

Conclusion

AI tools are powerful allies in software development, but like any technology, they come with potential pitfalls. By understanding these challenges and taking proactive steps to address them, you can ensure that AI tools enhance your productivity without introducing unnecessary risks.

In the next chapter, we'll look toward the future of AI in software development, exploring trends and strategies to help you stay ahead in an ever-changing landscape.

7

The Future of AI in Software Development

Chapter 7: Staying Ahead—The Future of AI in Software Development

The rapid evolution of artificial intelligence has already transformed software development, and this is just the beginning. As AI tools become more sophisticated and integrated into development workflows, they will unlock new possibilities, streamline complex processes, and redefine what it means to be a software developer.

In this chapter, we'll explore emerging trends, potential future developments in AI for software development, and strategies to help you stay ahead in this ever-changing landscape.

Emerging Trends in AI for Software Development

1. Enhanced Context Awareness

AI tools are becoming increasingly adept at understanding the broader context of a project, not just the immediate code they analyze.

- **What It Means:** Future AI tools will analyze entire codebases, identify interdependencies, and make more accurate suggestions based on the project's overall structure and goals.
- **Impact on Developers:** Developers will receive more meaningful, project-specific recommendations, reducing the time spent adapting AI outputs to their unique requirements.

2. Deeper Integration with Development Workflows

AI tools are moving beyond standalone applications to become seamlessly embedded in development environments.

- **What It Means:** Expect tighter integration with IDEs, version control systems, CI/CD pipelines, and project management tools.
- **Impact on Developers:** This integration will create smoother workflows, where AI suggestions and insights appear naturally as part of your day-to-day activities.

3. AI for DevOps

The rise of AI in DevOps is already evident in areas like automated monitoring and deployment optimization.

- **What It Means:** AI will play a larger role in managing infrastructure, predicting system failures, and automating remediation tasks.
- **Impact on Developers:** Developers will spend less time on operational tasks, focusing more on building features and improving user experiences.

4. Increased Collaboration with AI

AI tools are evolving into collaborative partners, offering not just assistance but proactive guidance.

- **What It Means:** AI will act as a team member, participating in design discussions, suggesting architectural improvements, and even generating proof-of-concept implementations.
- **Impact on Developers:** Developers will interact with AI tools conversationally, leveraging them as co-creators rather than static utilities.

5. Advances in Responsible AI

As AI tools become more prevalent, ethical considerations and responsible usage will take center stage.

- **What It Means:** Developers will have access to AI tools that prioritize ethical coding practices, flag potential biases, and ensure compliance with regulations.
- **Impact on Developers:** Building ethical and inclusive software will become easier, with AI actively supporting responsible decision-making.

How Developers Can Stay Ahead

1. Embrace Lifelong Learning

AI and software development are constantly evolving, making continuous learning essential.

- **Strategies:**
- Follow industry news and trends through blogs, webinars, and conferences.
- Experiment with new tools and technologies regularly.
- Invest in courses or certifications on AI and its applications in development.

2. Focus on Problem-Solving and Creativity

While AI excels at automation, creativity and complex problem-solving remain human strengths.

- **Strategies:**
- Practice breaking down complex problems into solvable components.
- Develop skills in areas where AI struggles, such as architectural design and innovative feature development.

3. Build AI Literacy

Understanding how AI works and its underlying principles will give you an edge in using it effectively.

- **Strategies:**
- Learn the basics of machine learning, natural language processing, and AI ethics.
- Explore how AI tools are trained and what limitations they

might have.

4. Collaborate with AI Responsibly

As AI tools become more integrated into workflows, under-standing their limitations and ensuring responsible usage will be critical.

- **Strategies:**
- Regularly review AI-generated outputs for accuracy and compliance with best practices.
- Advocate for ethical AI usage in your team or organization.

5. Network with the Community

Engaging with other developers can help you stay informed and learn from their experiences.

- **Strategies:**
- Join online forums, communities, or local meetups focused on AI in software development.
- Share your findings, challenges, and successes to contribute to collective learning.

Future Possibilities: What's Next for AI in Development?

1. AI-Driven Pair Programming

- AI tools may evolve into real-time pair programming part-ners, working alongside developers to brainstorm solutions, write code, and review outputs collaboratively.

2. Adaptive Learning AI Tools

- Future AI tools could adapt to individual developers' styles, preferences, and habits, providing hyper-personalized suggestions and insights.

3. Full Lifecycle Automation

- AI could manage the entire software development lifecycle, from planning and coding to testing and deployment, with minimal human intervention.

4. Cross-Domain Expertise

- AI tools will integrate knowledge from multiple domains, enabling them to suggest solutions that consider broader business or operational contexts.

Conclusion

The future of AI in software development is bright, with innovations on the horizon that will empower developers and redefine workflows. Staying ahead means embracing change, cultivating adaptability, and continually sharpening your skills. By positioning yourself as a proactive learner and responsible AI user, you can thrive in this rapidly evolving landscape and contribute to building the next generation of intelligent, efficient software.

8

Simulating Realistic Workflows with AI

Chapter 8: Simulating Realistic Workflows with AI

AI tools are most valuable when seamlessly integrated into day-to-day workflows. To understand their practical benefits, let's explore how these tools can be applied to common software development tasks. This chapter dives deep into four workflows, providing step-by-step scenarios to demonstrate how AI tools can enhance productivity and improve outcomes.

Workflow 1: Using AI for Feature Development

Scenario:

You're tasked with building a new feature for a web application: a user feedback form. The form will collect user input (name, email, and feedback message) and store the data in a database, with basic validation to ensure data integrity.

Step-by-Step Workflow:

Planning the Feature:

- **Task Breakdown:** Define the requirements:
- Fields: Name, Email, Feedback Message.
- Validation: Ensure all fields are required, email format is valid, and the message does not exceed 500 characters.
- Database: Save data in a table named feedback.
- **AI Assistance:** Use an AI tool like ChatGPT to outline the feature. Prompt:
- *"What components are needed to implement a feedback form with Flask? Include form validation and database storage."*
- The AI generates a checklist, ensuring nothing is overlooked.

Code Generation with AI:

- Open your IDE with GitHub Copilot enabled.
- Add a comment:
- *"# Flask route for handling feedback form submission with validation and database storage."*

Copilot generates boilerplate code:

```
@app.route('/submit_feedback', methods=['POST'])
def submit_feedback():
  data = request.json
  if not data.get('name') or not data.get('email') or
  not data.get('message'):
    return jsonify({'error': 'All fields are
    required'}), 400
  if len(data['message']) > 500:
    return jsonify({'error': 'Message too long'}), 400
```

```
# Save to database
conn = sqlite3.connect('feedback.db')
cursor = conn.cursor()
cursor.execute("INSERT INTO feedback (name, email,
message) VALUES (?, ?, ?)",
        (data['name'], data['email'],
        data['message']))
conn.commit()
conn.close()
return jsonify({'message': 'Feedback submitted
successfully'}), 200
```

Refinement:

- Review the generated code for accuracy. Adjust for your project's specific requirements (e.g., replacing SQLite with your preferred database).

Testing:

- Generate unit tests for the route using an AI tool:
- Prompt: *"Write unit tests for a Flask route that accepts feedback form data with validation."*
- The AI provides test cases for valid input, missing fields, invalid email format, and overly long messages.

Deployment and Verification:

- Deploy the feature to a staging environment.
- Use an AI testing tool to simulate various user inputs, ensuring the feature handles edge cases correctly.

Outcome:

You've implemented a fully functional, validated feedback form in a fraction of the time it would take manually.

Workflow 2: Debugging a Complex Issue with AI Assistance

Scenario:

Your real-time chat application encounters a race condition that causes sporadic message delivery failures when multiple users send messages simultaneously.

Step-by-Step Workflow:

Reproduce the Issue:

- Simulate a scenario where multiple users send messages concurrently. Collect error logs showing failed message deliveries.

Analyze with AI:

- Use a debugging tool like ChatGPT:
- Paste the error logs and a description:
- *"The chat app fails to deliver messages under heavy load. Logs show intermittent connection timeout errors."*
- The AI suggests possible causes:
- Insufficient connection pool size.
- Improper thread synchronization in the message queue handler.

Pinpoint the Problem:

- Use an AI-powered performance monitoring tool to identify bottlenecks in real time. The tool highlights excessive locking contention in the send_message function.

Fix the Issue:

- Implement AI-suggested changes:
- Increase connection pool size.
- Refactor the message queue handler to use asynchronous processing.
- AI tools like Copilot can assist in generating refactored code snippets.

Validate the Solution:

- Use an AI testing tool to simulate heavy traffic, ensuring the fix resolves the issue under various conditions.

Outcome:
You identify and resolve the bug efficiently, minimizing downtime and ensuring stable performance during peak usage.

Workflow 3: Writing and Optimizing Unit Tests with AI

Scenario:
You've developed a discount calculation feature for an e-commerce platform and need to ensure it handles all scenarios, including edge cases.
Step-by-Step Workflow:
Review Feature Logic:

- Feature functionality:
- Input: Product price, discount percentage, and user category.
- Output: Final price after applying discounts.
- AI Insight: Use ChatGPT to review the feature and identify potential edge cases:
- Zero discount.
- 100% discount.
- Negative prices or invalid inputs.

Generate Unit Tests:

- Prompt an AI tool:
- *"Write unit tests for a function that calculates discounts, covering edge cases like invalid inputs and maximum discounts."*

The AI generates test cases:

```
def test_calculate_discount():
  assert calculate_discount(100, 20) == 80
  assert calculate_discount(100, 0) == 100
  assert calculate_discount(100, 100) == 0
  with pytest.raises(ValueError):
    calculate_discount(-100, 20)
```

Optimize Test Coverage:

- Use an AI analysis tool to identify gaps in your tests (e.g., scenarios with multiple discounts or unusual user categories).

Execute and Review:

- Run the tests and use AI-powered debugging tools to analyze failures, if any.

Outcome:
Comprehensive, high-quality unit tests ensure robust functionality, reducing the likelihood of production bugs.

Workflow 4: Reviewing and Refactoring Code with AI Tools

Scenario:
You inherit a legacy codebase with inconsistent formatting,
duplicated logic, and inefficiencies. Your goal is to clean it up
for better maintainability.
  Step-by-Step Workflow:
  Scan the Codebase:

- Use a tool like DeepCode to analyze the codebase for issues.
  The tool identifies:
- Duplicated functions.
- Inefficient nested loops.
- Outdated library usage.

Review Suggestions:

- DeepCode recommends:
- Consolidating duplicate logic into a single reusable function.
- Replacing nested loops with list comprehensions for better

performance.

Refactor with AI Assistance:

- Use GitHub Copilot to refactor the flagged sections. For example:

Original code:

```
for i in range(len(numbers)):
  for j in range(len(numbers)):
    if numbers[i] == numbers[j]:
      print(numbers[i])
```

AI-suggested refactor:

```
for num in set(numbers):
  print(num)
```

1. **Validate Changes:**

- Generate test cases to confirm that refactored code maintains functionality.
- Use AI tools to simulate different scenarios and ensure no regressions.

Outcome:
The codebase becomes cleaner, faster, and easier to maintain,

improving the team's productivity and reducing technical debt.

Conclusion

By integrating AI tools into realistic workflows, you can see their tangible benefits in feature development, debugging, testing, and refactoring. These workflows highlight how AI enhances productivity, ensures higher-quality outputs, and reduces the burden of repetitive tasks. As you adopt and refine these workflows, AI will become an invaluable partner in your software development journey.

9

Conclusion

Conclusion: Maximizing AI in Your Workflow

Artificial intelligence has undeniably become a transformative force in software development. From generating boilerplate code to debugging complex issues, AI tools empower developers to focus on innovation while automating repetitive tasks. As we conclude this journey into the best practices and practical uses of AI in software development, let's recap the key takeaways, encourage experimentation, and look forward to a future where AI enhances creativity and productivity.

Key Takeaways

1. **AI Is a Partner, Not a Replacement:** AI tools are designed to augment human capabilities, not replace them. By automating routine tasks, AI allows developers to focus on problem-solving, design, and innovation.

2. **Versatility Across Tasks:** AI tools excel in diverse areas, from feature development and debugging to testing and code reviews. Whether you're a beginner or an experienced developer, these tools can adapt to your needs.

3. **The Importance of Responsible Use:** Responsible AI usage involves validating outputs, understanding limitations, and ensuring compliance with ethical and security standards. This approach ensures high-quality, inclusive, and secure software.

4. **Adaptability Is Key:** The right tool for one project may not be ideal for another. Understanding your specific requirements and evaluating tools accordingly is critical to maximizing their potential.

5. **Continuous Learning:** Staying ahead in a rapidly evolving landscape means embracing lifelong learning. Developers who understand and adapt to AI trends will remain indispensable in their fields.

Encouragement to Experiment

Every development team has unique workflows, challenges, and goals. The true value of AI lies in its adaptability—there's no one-size-fits-all solution. Here are some ways to experiment with AI tools to find what works best for you:

- **Start Small:** Integrate AI tools into specific tasks or projects to gauge their effectiveness.
- **Iterate and Learn:** Use feedback from your team and projects to refine how AI tools are used.

- **Explore New Features:** Many tools are frequently updated with new capabilities. Stay curious and explore these improvements to get the most out of your tools.
- **Collaborate with AI:** Treat AI tools as team members. Engage with their suggestions, adapt them to fit your project, and use them as springboards for creative ideas.

Final Thoughts

Embracing AI in software development is not just about improving productivity—it's about reimagining how we work. AI tools open doors to new possibilities, enabling developers to approach problems with enhanced creativity and efficiency. By automating the mundane and simplifying the complex, AI frees us to focus on building solutions that matter.

As you integrate AI into your workflow, remember that the tools are just one part of the equation. Your skills, judgment, and creativity remain central to the software development process. Together, AI and developers can create software that is not only functional but transformative.

The future of software development is collaborative, and AI is a partner that will evolve alongside us. By experimenting, adapting, and staying curious, you'll be well-equipped to thrive in this exciting era of innovation.

Thank you for taking this journey into the world of AI-powered software development. The tools, practices, and insights shared here are just the beginning. The rest is up to you—embrace AI, make it your own, and let it amplify your creativity and productivity in ways you never imagined.

AI Disclaimer

This book was created with the assistance of AI tools, including ChatGPT, to enhance the writing process. While every effort has been made to ensure the accuracy, relevance, and clarity of the content, the author has reviewed and refined all material to ensure it aligns with the intended purpose and audience. The AI-assisted approach reflects the very principles discussed in this book: leveraging technology to improve efficiency and creativity while maintaining the human touch.